United States Government Accountability Office

Report to Congressional Committees

December 2013

SMALL BUSINESS LENDING FUND

Treasury Should Ensure Evaluation Includes Methods to Isolate Program Impact

GAO Highlights

Highlights of GAO-14-135, a report to congressional committees

SMALL BUSINESS LENDING FUND

Treasury Should Ensure Evaluation Includes Methods to Isolate Program Impact

Why GAO Did This Study

The Small Business Jobs Act of 2010 aimed to stimulate job growth by, among other things, establishing the SBLF program within Treasury. SBLF was authorized to make up to $30 billion in capital investments to encourage banks and community development loan funds with assets of less than $10 billion to increase their small business lending. The act generally defined "small business lending" as loans not more than $10 million originally. Under the act, GAO is mandated to conduct an audit of SBLF annually. GAO's first and second reports were on the program's implementation and performance reporting and made recommendations on management oversight, program evaluation, and performance reporting. This third report examines (1) the growth in qualified small business lending and reasons for variations in the growth at SBLF banks and (2) actions Treasury has taken to evaluate participant lending patterns. GAO analyzed the most recent available performance and financial information on SBLF participants; reviewed government and private sector surveys on small business credit conditions; and interviewed officials from Treasury and representatives from SBLF participants.

What GAO Recommends

Treasury should follow through in conducting an impact evaluation that includes methods to isolate the effect of SBLF from other factors on participants' small business lending. In written comments on a draft of this report, Treasury agreed to implement the recommendation.

View GAO-14-135. For more information, contact Daniel Garcia-Diaz at (202) 512-8678 or garciadiazd@gao.gov.

What GAO Found

According to the U.S. Department of the Treasury (Treasury), as of June 30, 2013, Small Business Lending Fund (SBLF) participants had increased their qualified small business lending by $10.4 billion over their aggregate 2010 baseline of $36.5 billion. However, SBLF participants varied greatly in the extent to which they had increased small business lending. GAO analysis for the quarter ending June 30, 2013, showed that the median SBLF bank in the top (first) quartile had over a 100 percent increase over the baseline, compared to a 9.1 percent increase for the median SBLF bank in the bottom (fourth) quartile. Several factors GAO analyzed could help explain this variation. For example, the median bank in the bottom quartile had more troubled loans than banks in the top quartile, which could affect a bank's lending capacity. Also, a majority of banks in the bottom lending quartile used much of their SBLF funds to repay investments received from Treasury's Capital Purchase Program, leaving them with a much smaller net increase in available capital. Several banks GAO interviewed said that they have seen increased demand for credit as the economy improved. In addition, publicly reported surveys indicate that credit conditions have improved, but some small businesses continue to face challenges securing credit.

Median Changes in SBLF Banks' Qualified Small Business Lending by Quartile, June 30, 2013
Percentage growth

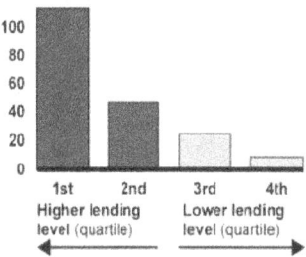

Source: GAO analysis of Treasury data

Note: SBLF banks in the first quartile had the highest levels of qualified small business lending and the most growth in small business lending compared to SBLF banks in the other three quartiles.

Treasury has taken steps to assess SBLF participants' lending patterns, including conducting a peer-group analysis and collecting performance data through an annual survey of SBLF participants. However, these steps are not sufficient to isolate the net impact of SBLF on participants' lending. Treasury officials said that they are exploring evaluation approaches and have a firm under contract to help identify statistical analyses that could be used, but have not provided documentation of its evaluation plan committing to an approach. GAO guidance on program evaluation suggests that impact evaluations are usually required to assess the net impact of a program by comparing the observed outcomes to an estimate of what would have happened in the program's absence. By conducting an evaluation that includes methods to assess the net impact of SBLF, Treasury could more effectively inform the public and Congress on how SBLF has affected the participants' lending compared to other factors, such as economic conditions, and could better assist Congress in making future decisions about similar capital investment programs or alternative programs that support small business access to capital.

_____ United States Government Accountability Office

Contents

Abbreviations

CAMELS	capital adequacy, asset quality, management, earnings, liquidity, and sensitivity to market risk
CDLF	community development loan funds
CPP	Capital Purchase Program
FDIC	Federal Deposit Insurance Corporation
Federal Reserve	Board of Governors of the Federal Reserve System
NFIB	National Federation of Independent Business
OCC	Office of the Comptroller of the Currency
SBLF	Small Business Lending Fund
TARP	Troubled Asset Relief Program

GAO
U.S. GOVERNMENT ACCOUNTABILITY OFFICE

441 G St. N.W.
Washington, DC 20548

December 11, 2013

Congressional Committees

In response to concerns about challenges faced by small businesses in recent years, Congress enacted the Small Business Jobs Act of 2010, which authorized the Secretary of the Department of the Treasury (Treasury) to make up to $30 billion of capital available and offered incentives to financial institutions to increase small business lending.[1] Among other things, the law aimed to stimulate job growth by establishing the Small Business Lending Fund (SBLF) to encourage financial institutions with assets of less than $10 billion to increase their lending to small businesses with up to $50 million in annual revenues. In 2011, 935 financial institutions applied to the program for a combined funding request of $11.7 billion. By September 2011, Treasury had approved $4 billion for 332 institutions through Treasury purchases of preferred stock or debt instruments. Of this $4 billion, $3.9 billion went to 281 banks and $104 million to 51 community development loan funds (CDLF).[2] No additional SBLF funds will be awarded to financial institutions.

The 2010 Small Business Jobs Act mandates us to conduct an annual audit of the SBLF program.[3] In our first and second reports, we reviewed the implementation of SBLF and made recommendations to improve the program's management oversight, program evaluation, and performance reporting.[4] This third report examines (1) the status of SBLF; (2) identified reasons for variation in growth of qualified small business lending at SBLF banks; and (3) actions Treasury has taken to evaluate SBLF participant lending patterns.

---

[1]Pub. L. No. 111-240, § 4103, 124 Stat. 2504, 2585 (codified at 12 U.S.C. § 4741).

[2]In this report "banks" refers to banks, thrifts, and bank and thrift holding companies. For purposes of the SBLF program, a CDLF is an entity that is certified by Treasury as a community development financial institution (CDFI) loan fund . A CDFI is a specialized financial institution that works in market niches that are underserved by traditional financial institutions.

[3]§ 4107(c), 124 Stat. at 2594 (codified at 12 U.S.C. § 4741).

[4]GAO, *Small Business Lending Fund: Additional Actions Needed to Improve Transparency and Accountability*, GAO-12-183 (Washington, D.C.: Dec. 14, 2011) and *Small Business Lending: Opportunities Exist to Improve Performance Reporting of Treasury's Programs*, GAO-13-76 (Washington, D.C.: Dec. 5, 2012).

To examine program status, including participants' lending, and dividend and interest payments, we reviewed Treasury data as of June 30, 2013, and Treasury's July and October 2013 Lending Growth Reports.[5] We also interviewed Treasury officials. To examine the process for exiting the program and participants' reasons for exiting, we collected documents and interviewed officials from Treasury and three bank regulatory agencies: the Office of the Comptroller of the Currency (OCC), the Board of Governors of the Federal Reserve System (Federal Reserve), and the Federal Deposit Insurance Corporation (FDIC). We spoke to these bank regulators to obtain information about their role in approving SBLF redemptions. Sixteen participants had left the program as of July 1, 2013. Six of these participants told Treasury the reasons why they were leaving the program. We contacted the other 10 participants that had left the program and had not shared their reasons for leaving with Treasury, and obtained responses from 9. To determine what is known about the reasons for variation in growth of small business lending at SBLF banks, we relied on Treasury's Lending Growth Report to divide 265 banks into four quartiles based on their level of qualified small business lending as of June 30, 2013, and compared the four quartiles to one another using financial and regulatory data, including Call Report data and CAMELS composite ratings.[6] We accessed Call Report data of SBLF banks using SNL Financial—a company that manages a financial database containing publicly filed regulatory and financial reports—and analyzed data such as asset size, Texas Ratios, and net SBLF capital received, among other variables, as a way to assess the factors associated with different lending levels.[7] We also analyzed CAMELS composite ratings from FDIC to

---

[5]The Lending Growth Report is Treasury's quarterly report to Congress descr bing how participating SBLF institutions have used the funds they have received under the program. Prior to the October 2013 report, these reports were titled Use of Funds Report.

[6]SBLF banks in the first quartile had the highest levels of qualified small business lending and the most growth in small business lending compared to SBLF banks in the other three quartiles.

[7]A Call Report is the common reference name for the quarterly reports of condition and income filed with regulators by every national bank, state-chartered Federal Reserve member bank, and insured state nonmember bank. The Texas Ratio is defined as nonperforming assets ("troubled loans") plus loans 90 or more days past due divided by tangible equity and reserves. The observations in the dataset are banks participating in SBLF or their subsidiaries with available financial data.

GAO-14-135 Small Business Lending Fund

determine if there was variation across the quartiles of SBLF banks.[8] In addition, we performed a regression analysis to simultaneously control for multiple aspects of SBLF banks' financial condition, as well as to attempt to account for state-level economic conditions. To describe the reasons why some SBLF banks were more or less successful in increasing lending to small businesses, we also selected and attempted to contact a nonprobability, judgmental sample of 12 banks based on geographic distribution and participation in Treasury's Capital Purchase Program (CPP), and we obtained responses from 10 of them.[9] We also interviewed Treasury officials responsible for the program and contacted representatives of the National Federation of Independent Business, because it regularly surveys small businesses, and the American Bankers Association and Independent Community Bankers Association, because they represent the interests of community banks. We also used a number of other survey indicators that provide a variety of perspectives on small business credit market conditions. We assessed the reliability of the data used for our analyses by, for example, inspecting data for missing observations and outliers and reviewing prior GAO work and updating information as appropriate. We determined that the data collected by Treasury, FDIC, and SNL Financial and the survey indicators we reviewed were sufficiently reliable for our purposes of providing a high-level overview of the program status and variations of changes in SBLF banks' qualified small business lending. To determine actions Treasury has taken to evaluate SBLF participant lending patterns, we reviewed Treasury's Lending Growth Reports issued in October 2012, and January, April, July and October 2013, and its first annual lending survey instrument and results report, as well as relevant supporting

---

[8]The CAMELS rating system is a U.S. supervisory tool that describes a bank's overall condition and that is used to classify the nation's banks. The composite rating is based on financial statements and regulators' on-site examinations and has six components—capital adequacy, asset quality, management, earnings, liquidity, and sensitivity to market risk—that make up the acronym. It rates banks on a scale of 1 to 5, with 1 being the strongest. Evaluations of the six CAMELS components take into consideration a bank's size and sophistication, the nature and complexity of its banking activities, and its risk profile.

[9]As the largest capital infusion program under the Troubled Asset Relief Program, CPP was designed to provide capital investments to financially viable financial institutions. Treasury received preferred shares and subordinated debentures, along with warrants.

documentation of these reports.[10] We interviewed Treasury officials to understand the agency's efforts to assess program performance. We also reviewed our 2011 and 2012 reports on SBLF to document Treasury's past efforts in assessing SBLF performance. Furthermore, we reviewed GAO guidance on program evaluation and past GAO work on federal government performance management, and compared them with Treasury actions.[11] In addition, we reviewed impact evaluations conducted by GAO and other federal agencies to enhance our understanding and provide examples of impact evaluations and statistical techniques.[12] See appendix I for a more detailed discussion of our scope and methodology.

We conducted this performance audit from March 2013 to December 2013 in accordance with generally accepted government auditing standards. Those standards require that we plan and perform the audit to obtain sufficient, appropriate evidence to provide a reasonable basis for our findings and conclusions based on our audit objectives. We believe that the evidence obtained provides a reasonable basis for our findings and conclusions based on our audit objectives.

---

[10]The SBLF lending survey is an annual survey required by Treasury for all SBLF participants as part of the agreement between Treasury and SBLF participants. The first annual survey covered from July 1, 2011, to June 30, 2012.

[11]See GAO, *Program Evaluation: A Variety of Rigorous Methods Can Help Identify Effective Interventions*, GAO-10-30 (Washington, D.C.: Nov. 23, 2009); *Performance Measurement and Evaluation: Definitions and Relationships*, GAO-11-646SP (Washington, D.C.: May 2011); *Designing Evaluations: 2012 Revision*, GAO-12-208G (Washington, D.C.: January 2012); and *Program Evaluation: Strategies to Facilitate Agencies' Use of Evaluation in Program Management and Policy Making*, GAO-13-570 (Washington, D.C.: June 26, 2013).

[12]See GAO, *Tax Policy: New Markets Tax Credit Appears to Increase Investment by Investors in Low-Income Communities, but Opportunities Exist to Better Monitor Compliance*, GAO-07-296 (Washington, D.C.: Jan. 31, 2007); Social Policy Research Associates and Mathematica Policy Research, Inc., *Estimated Impacts for Participants in the Trade Adjustment Assistance (TAA) Program Under the 2002 Amendments* (August 2012); Urban Institute Justice Policy Center, *The Multi-Site Adult Drug Court Evaluation: The Impact of Drug Courts* (November 2011); and Institute of Education Sciences and Mathematical Policy Research, *Impacts of Title I Supplemental Educational Services on Student Achievement* (May 2012).

Background

The Small Business Jobs Act of 2010 defines qualified small business lending—as defined by and reported in an institution's quarterly regulatory filings, also known as Call Reports—as one of the following:

- commercial and industrial loans;
- owner-occupied nonfarm, nonresidential real-estate loans;
- loans to finance agricultural production and other loans to farmers; and
- loans secured by farmland.

In addition, qualifying small business loans cannot be for an original amount of more than $10 million, and the business may not have more than $50 million in revenue. The act specifically prohibits Treasury from accepting applications from institutions that are on FDIC's problem bank list or have been removed from that list during the previous 90 days. The initial baseline small business lending amount for the SBLF program was the average amount of qualified small business lending that was outstanding for the four full quarters ending on June 30, 2010, and the dividend or interest rates paid by an institution are adjusted by comparing future lending against this baseline. Also, the institution is required to report any loans resulting from purchases, mergers, and acquisitions so that its qualified small business lending baseline is adjusted accordingly.

Fewer institutions applied to SBLF than were initially anticipated, in part because many banks did not anticipate that demand for small business loans would increase. The institutions that applied to and were funded by SBLF were primarily institutions with total assets of less than $500 million. In addition, in our 2011 report, we found that the lack of clarity by Treasury in explaining the program's requirements created confusion among applicants and that Treasury faced multiple delays in implementing the SBLF program and disbursing SBLF funds by the statutory deadline of September 27, 2011.[13] We recommended Treasury apply lessons learned from the application review phase of SBLF to help improve its communications with SBLF participants and other interested stakeholders, such as Congress and bank regulators. In 2012, in response to our recommendation, Treasury officials said that they had enhanced their communication strategy with SBLF participants and

---

[13]GAO-12-183.

stakeholders and developed written communication guidelines to provide for consistency, continuity, and validity.

The amount of funding an institution received under the SBLF program depended on its asset size as of the end of the fourth quarter of calendar year 2009. Specifically, if the qualifying financial institution had total assets of $1 billion or less, it was eligible for SBLF funding that equaled up to 5 percent of its risk-weighted assets. If the qualifying institution had assets of more than $1 billion but less than $10 billion, it was eligible for funding that equaled up to 3 percent of its risk-weighted assets. In the case of bank or thrift holding companies, assets were to be measured based on the total combined assets of the insured depository institution subsidiaries and risk-weighted assets were to be measured based on the combined risk-weighted assets of the insured depository institution subsidiaries. The SBLF program provided an option for eligible institutions to refinance preferred stock or subordinated debt issued to Treasury through CPP. At the time of application, the institution was required to submit a small business lending plan to its regulator describing how the applicant's business strategy and operating goals will allow it to address the needs of small businesses in the area it serves.

Participating SBLF C-corporation banks and bank holding companies pay dividends of up to 5 percent per year initially to Treasury, with reduced rates available if they increase their small business lending.[14] The initial dividend rate is based on the difference between the baseline level and the lending reported in the second calendar quarter preceding the SBLF closing date. Additionally, the dividend rate payable decreases quarterly as banks increase small business lending over their baselines. While the dividend rate was no more than 5 percent for the first 9 quarters (a little over 2 years), a bank could reduce the rate to 1 percent by generating a 10 percent increase in its lending to small businesses compared with its baseline. After 9 quarters, the dividend rate on the capital became fixed at the rate the participating banks were paying at that time if they had increased their small business lending; otherwise, the dividend rate increased to 7 percent if participating banks had not increased their small business lending. After 4.5 years, the dividend rate on the capital

---

[14]Some banking institutions are formed as C-corporations. C-corporations pay federal and state income tax on earnings. When earnings are distributed to shareholders as dividends they are subject to taxation. C-corporations, unlike S-corporations, are taxed separately from their owners.

increases to 9 percent for all banks regardless of a bank's small business lending. For S-corporations and mutual institutions, the initial interest rate was at most 7.7 percent. The rate fell as low as 1.5 percent for the institutions that increased their small business lending by 10 percent or more from the previous quarter.[15] For CDLFs, the initial dividend rate is 2 percent for the first 8 years. After 8 years, the rate increases to 9 percent if the CDLF has not repaid the SBLF funding. This structure is designed to encourage CDLFs to repay the capital investment by the end of the 8-year period. Treasury allows an SBLF participant to exit the program at any time, with the approval of its regulator, by repaying the funding provided along with dividends owed for that period.

Under the act, Treasury has a number of reporting requirements to Congress related to SBLF: (1) monthly reports describing all of the transactions made under the program during the reporting period; (2) a semiannual report (for the periods ending each March and September) providing all projected costs and liabilities and all operating expenses; and (3) a quarterly report, known as the Lending Growth Report, detailing how participants have used the funds they have received under the program.

---

[15]Some banking institutions are formed as S-corporations. S-corporations elect not to pay income tax. Instead the corporation's income or losses are divided among and passed through to shareholders. Some banking institutions are formed as mutual companies. A mutual company does not issue stock and therefore does not have shareholders. In mutual companies profits are set aside for the benefit of the depositors or are held as surplus reserves to maintain liquidity.

SBLF-Funded Participants Continue to Lend to Small Businesses and Some Participants Have Left the Program

SBLF participants had increased lending over baseline levels as of June 30, 2013, according to Treasury's Lending Growth Report.[16] Total qualified small business lending for SBLF participants—banks and CDLFs—increased by almost $10.4 billion over their aggregate baseline of about $36.5 billion. Bank participants increased their qualified small business lending by about $10.1 billion over a baseline of about $35.7 billion. CDLFs increased their qualified small business lending by about $256.3 million over a baseline of about $796.8 million. Of the 265 participating banks, 246 (93 percent) increased their qualified small business lending, and 45 of the 50 CDLFs (90 percent) increased their qualified small business lending.

SBLF participants had made about $188 million in dividend or interest payments to Treasury as of June 30, 2013—$185 million from banks and $3 million from CDLFs. As of June 30, 2013, SBLF participants had not missed any payments. Figure 1 shows the numbers of program participants in different dividend or interest rate categories.

---

[16]As established by the act, the baseline for measuring the change in small business lending is the average of the amounts that were reported for each of the four calendar quarters which ended June 30, 2010.

Figure 1: Distribution of Dividend or Interest Rates Paid by Participants on SBLF Funds, as of June 30, 2013

Number of SBLF Participants

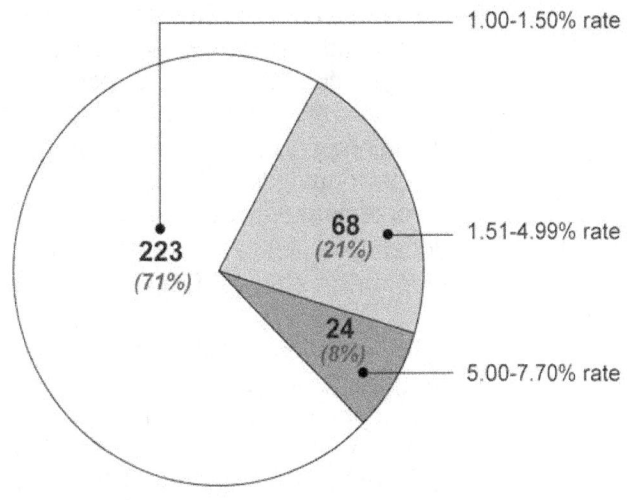

(%) = proportion of SBLF institutions paying that rate

Source: GAO analysis of Treasury data.

As of July 1, 2013, 16 participants with aggregate investments of $147.3 million had fully redeemed Treasury's investment. The structure of the SBLF program is designed to encourage banks to repay the capital investment by the end of 4.5 years and CDLFs to repay at the end of 8 years. However, Treasury allows an SBLF participant to exit the program at any time. SBLF securities may be redeemed at any time subject to the submission of a formal request to Treasury. Treasury reviews the notice to determine whether it meets a number of conditions. The redemption amount must equal at least 25 percent of the original funding balance. The redemption date must be no more than 60 days and no fewer than 30 days from the date the notice is sent to Treasury. Payment of accrued dividends or interest for the current dividend period must be made in addition to the principal balance.

Because exiting the SBLF program would affect a participant's capital, banks that want to leave the program also need approval from their appropriate federal banking regulator. If the SBLF participant is a bank or thrift, upon receipt of a redemption notice, Treasury notifies the appropriate federal banking regulator to determine if it has any objection. The federal banking regulator then reviews the redemption request to analyze the impact of the redemption of SBLF securities on capital levels. The analysis bank regulators perform for SBLF redemptions is similar to the analysis they would undertake for other banks and thrifts engaging in activities that would reduce their capital. In general, federal banking regulators assess whether banks will have sufficient capital after redeeming their SBLF securities and whether the banks have the financial ability or capital strength to exit the SBLF program. The decision is based in part on the bank's condition and the bank's capital planning process, including performance and leverage ratios, classified assets, nonperforming loans, allowance for loan and lease losses, outstanding enforcement actions, and other factors.[17] If the federal banking regulator does not object to the redemption, Treasury proceeds with the redemption after verifying that they meet requirements for redemption.

SBLF participants exited the program for a variety of reasons. Some participants shared with Treasury the reasons for leaving the program, though they are not required to do so. Four participants told Treasury that they wanted to redeem their SBLF securities prior to an acquisition by another bank. Another participant told Treasury it was redeeming SBLF securities due to a difficult economic environment and the potential impact of revised regulatory capital guidelines. Another participant said it wanted to eliminate ongoing dividend expenses and compliance costs associated with the SBLF program requirements. For those participants that did not provide a reason to Treasury, we contacted 10 former participants that fully repaid their SBLF funds to ask them their reasons for leaving the program. We received responses from nine participants and some gave multiple reasons for leaving. For example, eight participants told us that they exited the program to avoid dividend expenses and said that they could obtain less expensive funding elsewhere. Two participants told us that reporting and compliance were

---

[17]Classified assets are designated as "substandard," "doubtful," and "loss." A substandard asset is inadequately protected by the current sound worth and paying capacity of the obligor or of the collateral pledged, if any. Assets so classified must have a well-defined weakness or weaknesses that jeopardize the liquidation of the debt. They are characterized by the distinct possbility that the institution will sustain some loss if the deficiencies are not corrected. An asset classified doubtful has all the weaknesses inherent in one classified substandard with the added characteristic that the weaknesses make collection or liquidation in full, on the basis of currently existing facts, conditions, and values, highly questionable and improbable. Assets classified loss are considered uncollectible and of such little value that their continuance as bankable assets is not warranted.

burdensome, and officials from two banks said that demand for small business loans was not as strong as they had expected.

Several Factors Help Explain Variation in Small Business Lending Growth

Factors that help to explain the variation in qualified small business lending across SBLF banks include the condition of banks' loan portfolios, amount of net capital received from SBLF, and demand for credit, among others. In addition, our analysis of survey data indicates that credit is still difficult to obtain, although it has eased some compared with 2009. Further, while some banks confirmed to us that demand for credit has improved, some also said they face several challenges in increasing their qualified small business loan portfolios.

Certain Financial Conditions Affected Growth in Small Business Lending

To determine reasons for variation in small business lending among SBLF banks, we divided banks into four quartiles based on their level of qualified small business lending. We then analyzed financial conditions for each quartile to determine if differences in qualified small business lending could be explained in part by differences in financial conditions across the four quartiles.[18] We also performed a regression analysis to simultaneously control for multiple aspects of banks' financial condition, as well as to attempt to account for state-level economic conditions.[19] As shown in figure 2, SBLF banks in the first quartile increased qualified small business lending 114.1 percent over their baseline, compared to 47.6 percent for banks in the second quartile, 25 percent for banks in the third quartile, and 9.1 percent for banks in the fourth quartile, as of June 30, 2013.

[18]Qualified small business lending—lending below the $10 million threshold—is defined by the Small Business Jobs Act, and only SBLF participants are required to submit these data. We did not assess banks' individual financial condition; rather, we looked at the medians of certain indicators to make comparisons between the four quartiles. We analyzed financial characteristics of the four quartiles as of March 31, 2011, and June 30, 2013, to determine if any differences were associated with the initial financial condition of SBLF banks or changes in their financial condition that occurred during the program. Appendix I contains a more detailed description of our scope and methodology.

[19]A regression analysis can isolate the relationship between a variable and an outcome, accounting for the fact that other variables may also contribute to the outcome. For purposes of this report, the regression analysis can help determine which conditions, among those we were able to quantify, are most strongly associated with success at increasing qualified small business lending. See appendix II for more information.

Figure 2: Median Changes in SBLF Banks' Qualified Small Business Lending by Quartile, from Baseline Level to the Quarter Ending June 30, 2013

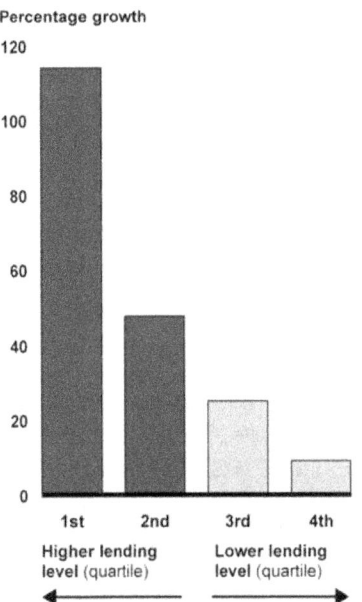

Percentage growth

Source: GAO analysis of Treasury data.

Note: SBLF banks in the first quartile had the highest levels of qualified small business lending and the most growth in small business lending compared to SBLF banks in the other three quartiles.

Our analysis of the financial condition of SBLF banks found that banks in the quartiles with lower levels of qualified small business lending had more troubled loans compared to those in the quartiles with higher lending levels, which may have negatively affected their ability to lend. As illustrated in figure 3, as of June 30, 2013, the median Texas Ratios increased across the four quartiles, with the first quartile having the lowest median Texas Ratio.[20] The Texas Ratio can indicate a bank's likelihood of failure by comparing its troubled loans to its capital. The higher the ratio, the more likely the institution is to fail because more of its capital could be eroded by realized losses on these troubled loans. We also found the Texas Ratio was higher for all banks prior to SBLF funding, which is to be expected because capital received under SBLF would tend to decrease the bank's Texas Ratio.

---

[20]As previously discussed, the Texas Ratio is defined as nonperforming assets ("troubled loans") plus loans 90 or more days past due divided by tangible equity and reserves.

GAO-14-135 Small Business Lending Fund

Figure 3: Median Texas Ratios across the Four Quartiles, as of June 30, 2013

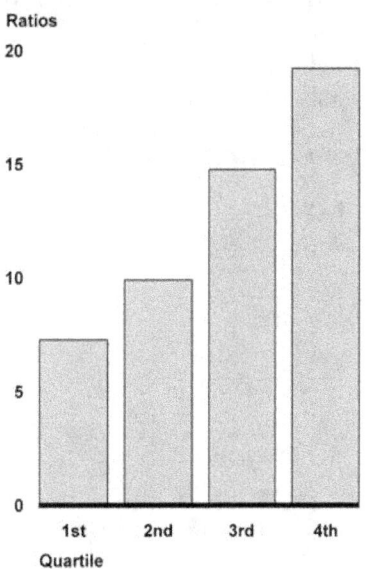

Source: GAO analysis of Treasury and SNL Financial data.

In addition, we also reviewed CAMELS composite ratings for each quartile as another factor that may have contributed to variation in lending but found minimal differences across the quartiles. Institutions were generally satisfactorily rated when approved for the program in 2011 because institutions with a CAMELS rating of either "4" or "5" were not allowed to participate in the program. On average, banks across the four quartiles as of March 31, 2011, and June 30, 2013, had similar median and average CAMELS ratings, ranging from 1.81 to 2.0. See appendix I for other indicators of financial health we analyzed, including measures of equity, asset liquidity, reliance on wholesale funding, and troubled loans.

Another factor associated with a bank's ability to increase qualified small business lending in the program is the amount of net SBLF capital received. Our analysis revealed that banks in the third and fourth quartiles had the lowest amount of net SBLF capital received. This trend can be at least partly explained by the fact that 67 percent of banks in the third quartile and 60 percent of banks in the fourth quartile were CPP participants and may have received only enough SBLF capital to repay

CPP funds (see fig. 4).[21] We identified several cases where banks in the third and fourth quartiles that converted through CPP either did not receive enough SBLF capital to repay CPP or received just enough funding to break even.[22] Hence, these banks did not receive any net SBLF capital to support increased qualified small business lending.[23]

Figure 4: Percentage of Capital Purchase Program (CPP) Participants by Quartile, as of June 30, 2013

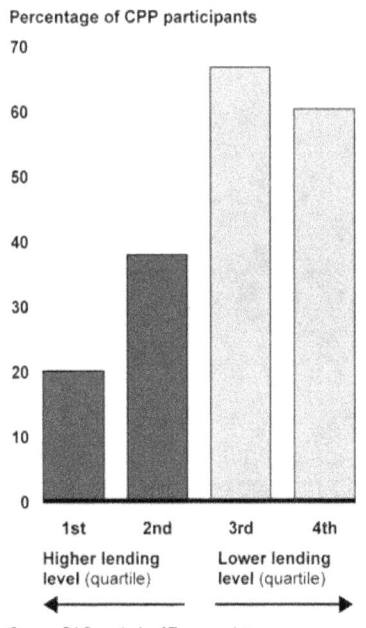

Percentage of CPP participants

1st / 2nd: Higher lending level (quartile)
3rd / 4th: Lower lending level (quartile)

Source: GAO analysis of Treasury data.

For all banks, we found a significant difference among the quartiles in net capital received as a percentage of assets, as of March 31, 2011 (see fig. 5). Specifically, for the median bank in the first quartile, SBLF net capital

---

[21]Approximately 46 percent of banks participating in SBLF refinanced preferred stock or subordinated debt issued to Treasury through CPP.

[22]While some SBLF banks may not have received enough SBLF capital to repay CPP, they could have exited the program by other means, such as repurchasing remaining preferred shares or subordinated debt. In addition, we found some SBLF banks exited CPP before participating in SBLF, that is, they did not rely on SBLF or another federal program to exit CPP.

[23]The initial capital that banks received from CPP was also intended to support lending.

GAO-14-135 Small Business Lending Fund

represented 2.9 percent of total assets compared to 2.2 percent for the median bank in the second quartile, 1.3 percent for the median bank in the third quartile, and 0.87 percent for the median bank in the fourth quartile. These differences may help explain the lower lending of banks in the fourth quartile, which our analysis found to have the highest median asset size. These banks had less net capital to support increased qualified small business lending because they were more likely to have converted through CPP. Although SBLF banks may not have received a large amount of additional capital to increase lending, the capital these institutions received through CPP was also intended to increase lending.

Figure 5: Median Net SBLF Capital Received as a Percentage of Assets, as of March 31, 2011

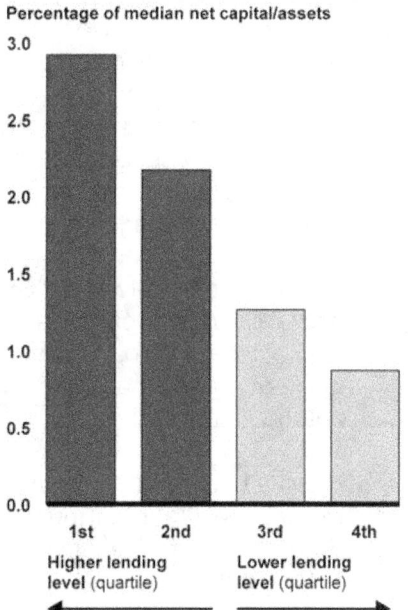

Percentage of median net capital/assets

Source: GAO analysis of Treasury and SNL Financial data.

Our regression analysis indicates that lower growth in qualified small business lending was associated with more troubled loans, greater leverage, less net capital received from SBLF, and lower reported demand for small business loans.[24] After controlling for net capital received, CPP status was no longer a statistically significant determinant of qualified small business lending growth. This result suggests that the lower lending at CPP institutions was driven in part by lower net capital rather than some other factor associated with prior CPP status that we did not observe. Our measure of state-level economic conditions—Gross Domestic Product growth—did not provide additional insight into any local economic conditions that might be driving differences in qualified small business lending. However, a participant-reported measure of demand for small business loans that was included in Treasury's survey of SBLF participants was a significant predictor of growth.[25] The magnitude of these various factors is summarized as follows:

- For every 14 percentage point increase in troubled loans (roughly one standard deviation) relative to capital and reserves, qualified small business lending growth decreased by 13 percentage points.

- For every 2 percentage points (roughly one standard deviation) more capital relative to assets (less leverage) prior to receiving SBLF capital, participants increased qualified small business lending by an additional 13 percentage points.

- A participant that received net SBLF capital of 1.9 percent (the mean) of assets relative to a participant that received no net capital (a potential outcome for participants that converted through CPP) increased qualified small business lending by an additional 18 percentage points.

- Participants that reported stronger demand for small business loans relative to those that reported weaker demand for small business loans increased qualified small business lending by an additional 24 percentage points.

---

[24]Leverage is broadly defined as the ratio between some measure of risk exposure and capital that can be used to absorb unexpected losses from the exposure. A highly leveraged bank could find it difficult to increase lending while maintaining a safe level of capital.

[25]Because demand was self-reported, we were unable to independently corroborate this variable. Participants with low growth in qualified small business lending may have had an incentive to report low demand to avoid the perception that they had underperformed.

GAO-14-135 Small Business Lending Fund

Credit Conditions and Other Factors Continue to Affect Banks' Ability to Lend

The SBLF program was designed to improve small businesses' access to credit, which had become difficult to obtain after the onset of the 2007-2009 recession. Based on our review of survey data and interviews with officials from 10 SBLF banks, factors that continue to affect small business lending include credit conditions and demand for small business loans, among others. Our analysis indicates that credit is still difficult to obtain, confirming that the lending environment remains challenging, although it has eased some compared with 2009. For example, according to the Wells Fargo/Gallup Small Business Index, as of the third quarter of 2013, 25 percent of businesses reported difficulty obtaining credit when they needed it compared to 33 percent in the third quarter of 2009.[26] Similarly, the Federal Reserve Senior Loan Officer Opinion Survey on Bank Lending Practices in July 2013 showed some large domestic banks having eased their credit standards.[27] Specifically, 90 percent of respondents reported that credit standards to small firms remained basically unchanged, and 10 percent reported that credit standards to small firms had eased somewhat. Some banks surveyed cited more aggressive competition from other banks or nonbank lenders as an important reason for easing standards or terms on loans. The conditions reported in the July 2013 survey improved from those reported in July 2009, when banks indicated they had continued to tighten standards on all major loan types.[28] Finally, the percentage of businesses whose borrowing needs were not satisfied improved from 10 percent in June 2009 to 5 percent in June 2013, while the percentage of businesses whose borrowing needs were satisfied was largely unchanged from June

---

[26]Wells Fargo conducts a survey of small businesses with a sample constructed by Gallup. Results of the third-quarter 2013 survey are based on telephone interviews with 602 small business owners, conducted July 22 through 26, 2013.

[27]The Federal Reserve Senior Loan Officer Opinion Survey surveys up to 80 large domestic banks and 24 U.S. branches and agencies of foreign banks. The July 2013 survey was based on the responses from 73 domestic banks and 22 U.S. branches and agencies of foreign banks. Large banks are defined as those with total domestic assets of $20 billion or more as of March 31, 2013. The survey addressed changes in the standards and terms on, and demand for, bank loans to businesses and households. Questions to respondents include whether lending standards and terms have tightened or eased for commercial and industrial loans to small, medium, and large firms. The survey asks respondents separately about their standards for and demand from large and middle-market firms, which are generally defined as firms with annual sales of $50 million or more, and small firms, those with annual sales of less than $50 million.

[28]The July 2009 survey results are based on responses from 55 domestic banks and 23 U.S. branches and agencies of foreign banks.

2009 to June 2013 according to the Small Business Economic Trends survey from the National Federation of Independent Business (NFIB).[29]

Banks generally report stronger demand for credit from small businesses compared to 2009 conditions, which could help explain why SBLF banks could increase their lending, but weaknesses exist. For example, as of July 2013, 61.4 percent of respondents of the Senior Loan Officer Opinion Survey reported that demand for commercial and industrial loans for small firms remained unchanged, and 30 percent reported moderately stronger demand for these loans. Conversely, as of July 2009, 34 percent of respondents reported that demand for commercial and industrial loans for small firms remained unchanged, and 52.8 percent reported moderately weaker demand (5.7 percent reported moderately stronger demand). Based on our analysis of SBLF banks and the results of Treasury's SBLF annual survey, banks with lower levels of qualified small business lending were more likely to report weaker demand (see fig. 6).[30] Overall, 46 percent of respondents to Treasury's survey reported stronger demand for credit compared to 14 percent reporting weaker demand. Respondents also reported a net increase in the number of inquiries from small business borrowers regarding the availability and terms of lending. A recent Federal Reserve study noted many of the same factors have affected small businesses' access to credit since the onset of the 2007-2009 recession.[31] Specifically, the study reflected that banks noted small business owners are not expanding as a result of weak sales and earnings, among other factors. However, banks also viewed small businesses as less creditworthy because small businesses do not have

---

[29]The NFIB Research Foundation has collected data on small business economic trends with quarterly surveys since 1974 and monthly surveys since 1986. The survey asks NFIB members about economic outlook, employment, earnings, sales, prices, credit conditions, interest rates, inventories, and capital outlays. Respondents are NFIB members, with nearly half of all respondents from firms with five or fewer employees. In previous work we found that the composition of NFIB survey respondents is broadly representative of the size distribution of firms in the United States. However, we found that the survey overrepresents some industries, including manufacturing and construction, while underrepresenting some skilled service industries. As such, respondents may not reflect the credit experiences of all firms in the economy.

[30]As mentioned previously, all active SBLF participants are required to respond to the SBLF annual survey.

[31]Federal Reserve Bank of Cleveland, "Why Small Business Lending Isn't What It Used to Be," Economic Commentary, August 14, 2013, accessed on August 15, 2013, http://www.clevelandfed.org/research/commentary/2013/2013-10.cfm.

the necessary collateral or cash flows at the same time that banks have increased their credit standards.

Figure 6: Percentage of SBLF Banks Reporting Weak Demand by Quartile, as of June 30, 2012

Percentage of banks reporting weak demand

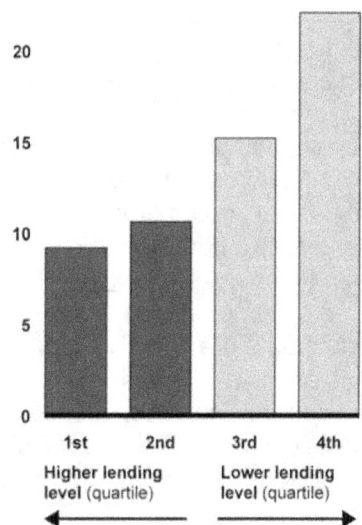

Source: GAO analysis of Treasury data.

We spoke with officials from 10 SBLF banks representing a range of success in increasing qualified small business lending, and they cited several reasons that they have had some success in increasing small business lending, as well as some challenges. Officials from five banks we interviewed across the quartiles attributed their lending growth to their ability to expand into new markets and hire additional loan officers. In addition, two banks cited strong loan growth in the agricultural, energy, and commercial and industrial sectors. Further, officials from some banks reported their customers are generally in better condition than they were a few years ago, but are uncomfortable taking on additional debt given the continued uncertainty around economic conditions and interest and tax rates. Officials from other banks cited difficulties based on their inability to compete with interest rates from larger banks and their local counterparts. Specifically, officials from four banks told us that while there are more creditworthy borrowers, there are more banks competing for these same borrowers. We also heard from officials at one bank that some small businesses in the area are less creditworthy than they used to be as a result of highly leveraged owner-occupied commercial real estate. Officials from the banks we interviewed that participated in CPP told us that they did so to obtain better dividend rates on the equity they received through SBLF.[32] One prior CPP participant told us that the bank's shareholders had a negative opinion of their participation in CPP, but had not raised any concerns since the bank had redeemed its shares through SBLF.

Treasury Has Taken Steps to Assess Performance and Is Exploring Program Evaluation Methods

Treasury has taken steps to assess SBLF participants' lending patterns, including collecting additional performance data and adopting additional analytical methods. Although actions taken to date do not represent an impact evaluation of SBLF, which would include analysis that isolates the impact of SBLF from other factors that affect small business lending, Treasury officials noted that they are exploring options to evaluate SBLF impact and are working with a contractor with expertise on statistical evaluation techniques. However, Treasury has not produced a written plan for completing the evaluation. By conducting an impact evaluation, Treasury could more effectively inform the public and Congress on how SBLF has affected the participants' lending compared to other factors, such as economic conditions, and could better assist Congress in making future decisions about similar capital investment programs or alternatives to such programs that support small businesses' access to capital.

Treasury Has Taken Steps to Assess SBLF Participants' Lending

Treasury has taken steps to assess SBLF program performance (participants' lending patterns) by including a peer-group analysis in the Lending Growth Reports and collecting additional performance information through annual surveys of program participants. In our December 2011 SBLF report, we recommended that Treasury finalize plans for assessing SBLF program performance.[33] Treasury explored different comparison methods in its Lending Growth Reports and in its January 2013 report added a peer-group comparison that mirrored the characteristics of SBLF participants more closely than the comparison

---

[32]In order to receive a better dividend rate in SBLF the bank had to increase qualified small business lending, otherwise the rates in SBLF were the same or higher than those in CPP.

[33]GAO-12-183.

group alone that Treasury had used in previous reports.[34] Treasury officials stated that they have considered additional options to evaluate the performance of SBLF and have included some of these in the Lending Growth Report. For example, they have included information on increases in lending following investment, increases in lending by financial condition, and additional loans based on annual survey results. However, they explored additional analyses using the peer-group comparison to review loan activity at the local level using census data but found this finer segmentation of loan data not available.

In addition, Treasury has collected additional performance information through an annual lending survey of SBLF participants. In 2012, Treasury initiated an annual survey of SBLF program participants and analyzed the survey results to obtain additional quantitative and qualitative data on how the program is performing. Treasury required that all active SBLF participants respond to the survey as part of the agreement to participate in the program. Treasury officials explained that while they collect information on the dollar amount of qualified small business loans at the end of each quarter, they intended to use the annual survey to supplement the quarterly data—such as by gathering additional information on the volume of the loans originated over time—and to provide additional information on how the participants are using SBLF funds. The survey covered several topics for the period from July 1, 2011, to June 30, 2012:

- changes in participants' small business lending standards and demand;
- obstacles to increasing small business lending;
- actual increases in small business lending by industry sector, number, and dollar value;
- actions associated with use of SBLF funds, including projected total increase in small business lending over 2 years; and

---

[34]According to Treasury's January 2013 Lending Growth Report, Treasury's peer group was composed of 543 non-SBLF banks that were selected to match the specific size, geography, and financial condition of SBLF banks; and its comparison group was comprised of 6,297 non-SBLF banks that were established prior to March 31, 2009, had total assets between $7.0 million and $6.4 billion (the range of total assets for SBLF participants) as of March 31, 2011 (the end of the first quarter prior to SBLF participants receiving funding), are located in one of the jurisdictions (44 states and the District of Columbia) in which SBLF participants are headquartered, and reported receiving a positive amount of business lending in the baseline period.

- small business outreach activities required by the Small Business Jobs Act of 2010.[35]

After receiving the survey responses from SBLF participants, Treasury analyzed the results of the SBLF annual survey and reported the aggregate results in June 2013.[36] The survey results report (1) provides Treasury's analysis of the aggregate survey results; (2) includes the results of each survey question; (3) discusses the methods Treasury followed to validate and review individual responses to each survey question for completeness and reasonableness; and (4) discusses the general methods Treasury used to review the aggregate survey results for reasonableness, including describing examples of the specific analyses for 9 of the 14 survey questions. For example, the report says that Treasury compared aggregate responses to six questions to similar questions related to credit standards and loan demand for commercial and industrial loans that are included in the Federal Reserve July 2012 Senior Loan Officer Opinion Survey and concluded that the SBLF aggregate results were reasonable. Treasury officials said they did not perform this type of analysis for some of the survey questions that were unique to SBLF, such as the question on participants' use of SBLF funding and questions related to outreach activities, because there was no appropriate data source to compare these aggregate responses.

Treasury officials explained that they have identified areas for improvement based on feedback obtained on the 2012 survey and made adjustments to the design and administration of the 2013 survey. Based on some questions from participants during the 2012 survey, Treasury provided additional guidance in responding to certain survey questions. In response to the questions and feedback, Treasury has refined some questions and is considering deleting and adding some questions to the 2013 survey. Treasury officials said they expect to continue to make adjustments to the survey in future years.

---

[35] Pub. L. No. 111-240, § 4103(d)(8), 124 Stat. 2504, 2591 (codified at 12 U.S.C. § 4741).

[36] U.S. Department of the Treasury, *Results of the First Annual SBLF Lending Survey*, June 2013.

Treasury Is Exploring Evaluation Methods but Has Not Yet Provided a Plan to Evaluate and Isolate the Program's Impact

Although Treasury has taken actions to improve its reporting and analysis of SBLF program performance, Treasury officials told us they recently started to review additional methods for evaluating the effectiveness of the program and its impact on participants' small business lending, but have not yet provided us with a plan to evaluate the program's impact or selected an approach for conducting the evaluation. Treasury's peer-group analysis in the Lending Growth Reports and the annual survey of program participants are valuable steps that contribute to an assessment of SBLF program performance. However, these actions are not sufficient to isolate the impact of SBLF on participants' lending compared to other factors—a component of performance measurement that we specifically highlighted in our 2011 and 2012 reports—which an impact evaluation could help to achieve. While we did not specifically recommend that Treasury conduct an impact evaluation in 2011, our recommendation that Treasury finalize plans for assessing SBLF performance noted that such plans should include measures that isolate the impact of the program. During our review, Treasury officials told us that they have started considering options to conduct a one-time evaluation of SBLF. For example, in October 2013, Treasury officials told us that since August 2013 they have been working with an existing contractor with expertise in statistical evaluation techniques to help plan and conduct the analysis, and that the contractor has begun to test out various techniques using available data. Treasury officials further explained that the evaluation will use data from September 30, 2013, when the dividend rate for most SBLF participants will become fixed, and the data will be available in November 2013.[37] Treasury officials stated that they intend to complete the analysis and publish the results in fiscal year 2014, but they had not yet provided us with a written plan for the evaluation committing to an approach.

According to GAO guidance on program evaluation, when a program is influenced by outside factors, as is the SBLF program, impact evaluations are usually required to assess the net effect of a program (or its actual effectiveness) by comparing the observed outcomes to an estimate of what would have happened in the program's absence.[38] The guidance

---

[37]As discussed in this report, 9 quarters (a little over 2 years) after the start of the SBLF program, SBLF participating banks, who had increased their small business lending, started to pay a fixed dividend rate based on the last quarter and those who had not increased lending would pay a fixed rate at 7 percent.

[38]GAO-12-208G and GAO-11-646SP.

further suggests that the design of an impact evaluation often includes using comparison groups and statistical tools and identifying the most important external influences on the desired program outcomes.[39] GAO and other federal agencies have conducted impact evaluations that have employed techniques, such as statistical tools, to isolate the impact of programs, and these could be useful examples for Treasury in designing its impact evaluation of SBLF.[40] All four evaluations included comparison groups in their evaluation design, while three of the four evaluations used a statistical tool known as propensity score matching—just one potential approach—in addition to other methods to consider in designing an impact evaluation of a program.[41] GAO has acknowledged that conducting program evaluations could be costly and time consuming— particularly collecting and ensuring the quality of data—and GAO guidance states that evaluators should aim to select the least burdensome way to obtain the information necessary to address the evaluation question.[42] Treasury already has existing performance information and has already demonstrated that it could readily obtain financial data on SBLF participants and their peers that have been regularly collected by third parties as it does for its peer analysis in the Lending Growth Report. An impact evaluation would help Treasury more effectively inform the public and Congress about how SBLF has affected the participants' lending compared to other factors, such as economic conditions. The impact evaluation would also provide useful information to Congress in designing future programs that use capital investments or in considering alternatives to SBLF that support small business access to capital.

---

[39]GAO-12-208G.

[40]See, for example, GAO-07-296; Social Policy Research Associates and Mathematica Policy Research, Inc., *Estimated Impacts*; Urban Institute Justice Policy Center, *The Multi-Site Adult Drug Court Evaluation*; and Institute of Education Sciences and Mathematical Policy Research, *Impacts of Title I Supplemental Educational Services*.

[41]Propensity score matching is a statistical technique used to model the variables that influence participants' assignment to the program and are then applied to the analysis of outcome data to reduce the influence of those variables on the program's estimated net impact.

[42]GAO-12-208G.

Conclusions

Treasury has continued to develop and refine its approach to assessing the performance of SBLF and measuring the extent to which SBLF participants have increased small business lending. However, these actions do not provide a clear picture of how SBLF has impacted participants' lending compared to other factors that could explain the increases in lending. Our guidance on program evaluation notes that impact evaluations are usually required to assess the net impact of a program by comparing the program outcomes to an estimate of what would have happened in the program's absence, often using statistical tools. Treasury officials have told us that they are exploring various approaches to evaluating the program and have a firm under contract that is helping to identify different statistical analyses that could be used. These actions are important initial steps in conducting an impact evaluation. Nevertheless, Treasury has not yet developed a written evaluation plan committed to a specific approach that would show that their evaluation assesses the net impact of SBLF apart from other factors. Given that capital investment programs had been used to address an immediate need during the recent financial crisis and policymakers may face similar changing economic conditions in the future and need to make quick decisions, it is important that Congress and other stakeholders have information about the performance of SBLF and the extent to which it had a meaningful impact on small business lending. An impact evaluation of SBLF would help provide critical information for decision makers, who will likely face another constrained credit environment for small business in the future and will seek options, such as a capital investment approach, or other approaches to promote small business credit, for addressing it.

Recommendation for Executive Action

To help ensure that Treasury can provide a useful assessment of SBLF that informs Congress and stakeholders of the effectiveness of this capital investment program in increasing lending, Treasury should follow through in conducting an impact evaluation of the program. In such an evaluation, Treasury should ensure that the analytical approaches identified by its contractor will isolate the role of SBLF from other factors that could affect small business lending to show the net impact of the program.

Agency Comments and Our Evaluation

We provided a draft of this report to Treasury, FDIC, the Federal Reserve and OCC for review and comment. Treasury provided written comments, which are reprinted in appendix III. FDIC, Federal Reserve, and OCC did not provide written comments on the draft report. In its written comments, Treasury agreed with our recommendation and stated that it will complete analysis using data from the conclusion of the program's two-year incentive period, which ended on September 30, 2013. It anticipates publishing the results of its evaluation in fiscal year 2014. Treasury stated that it will continue to explore analytical approaches that isolate SBLF's role from other factors affecting small business lending. Treasury also noted that the statistical technique of random assignment cannot be used to assess SBLF program impact and therefore unmeasured factors could account for differences in lending growth between participants and comparison groups. We agree that even powerful statistical techniques cannot perfectly replicate random assignment. However, these techniques can improve confidence in whether or not observed results are attributable to SBLF. Treasury and FDIC also provided technical comments on the draft report, which we've incorporated in the final report, as appropriate.

We are sending copies of this report to the appropriate congressional committees, Treasury, FDIC, the Federal Reserve, and OCC. The report also is available at no charge on the GAO website at http://www.gao.gov.

If you or your staff members have any questions about this report, please contact Daniel Garcia-Diaz at (202) 512-8678 or garciadiazd@gao.gov. Contact points for our Offices of Congressional Relations and Public Affairs may be found on the last page of this report. GAO staff who made major contributions to this report are listed in appendix IV.

Daniel Garcia-Diaz
Director
Financial Markets and Community Investment

List of Committees

The Honorable Debbie Stabenow
Chairwoman
The Honorable Thad Cochran
Ranking Member
Committee on Agriculture, Nutrition and Forestry
United States Senate

The Honorable Barbara Mikulski.
Chairwoman
The Honorable Richard Shelby
Vice Chairman
Committee on Appropriations
United States Senate

The Honorable Tim Johnson
Chairman
The Honorable Mike Crapo
Ranking Member
Committee on Banking, Housing, and Urban Affairs
United States Senate

The Honorable Patty Murray
Chairwoman
The Honorable Jeff Sessions
Ranking Member
Committee on the Budget
United States Senate

The Honorable Max Baucus
Chairman
The Honorable Orrin G. Hatch
Ranking Member
Committee on Finance
United States Senate

The Honorable Mary L. Landrieu
Chairwoman
The Honorable James E. Risch
Ranking Member
Committee on Small Business and Entrepreneurship
United States Senate

The Honorable Frank D. Lucas
Chairman
The Honorable Collin Peterson
Ranking Member
Committee on Agriculture
House of Representatives

The Honorable Harold Rogers
Chairman
The Honorable Nita M. Lowey
Ranking Member
Committee on Appropriations
House of Representatives

The Honorable Paul Ryan
Chairman
The Honorable Chris Van Hollen
Ranking Member
Committee on the Budget
House of Representatives

The Honorable Jeb Hensarling
Chairman
The Honorable Maxine Waters
Ranking Member
Committee on Financial Services
House of Representatives

The Honorable Sam Graves
Chairman
The Honorable Nydia Velázquez
Ranking Member
Committee on Small Business
House of Representatives

The Honorable Dave Camp
Chairman
The Honorable Sander Levin
Ranking Member
Committee on Ways and Means
House of Representatives

GAO-14-135 Small Business Lending Fund

Appendix I: Objectives, Scope, and Methodology

Our objectives were to examine (1) the status of the Small Business Lending Fund (SBLF); (2) identify reasons for variation in growth of qualified small business lending at SBLF banks; and (3) actions the Department of the Treasury (Treasury) has taken to evaluate SBLF participant lending patterns.

SBLF Program Status

To examine program status, including participants' lending, and dividend and interest payments, we reviewed Treasury data as of June 30, 2013, and Treasury's July and October 2013 Lending Growth Reports.[1] We also reviewed Treasury documents related to SBLF redemptions as of July 1, 2013, and interviewed Treasury officials about the reasons participants had left the program. We also interviewed officials from the Office of the Comptroller of the Currency (OCC), the Board of Governors of the Federal Reserve System (Federal Reserve), and the Federal Deposit Insurance Corporation (FDIC) on their role in approving SBLF redemptions and on the reasons why banks have left the program. All three of these bank regulators provided us documents describing their procedures for capital redemptions. Sixteen participants had left the program as of July 1, 2013. Six of these participants told Treasury the reasons why they were leaving the program. We contacted the other 10 participants that left the program and did not share their reasons for leaving with Treasury, and we obtained responses from 9. One participant did not respond to our contact attempts.

Reasons for Variation in Small Business Lending

To determine reasons for variation in growth of qualified small business lending at SBLF banks, we used the most current level of qualified small business lending as of June 30, 2013, reported in Treasury's October 2013 Lending Growth Report, to divide 265 banks into four quartiles based on their level of qualified small business lending and compared the four quartiles to one another using financial and regulatory data.[2] We did

---

[1] The Lending Growth Report is Treasury's quarterly report to Congress descr bing how participating SBLF institutions have used the funds they have received under the program. Prior to the October 2013 report, these reports were titled Use of Funds Report.

[2] Qualified small business lending—lending below the $10 million threshold—is defined by the Small Business Jobs Act of 2010, and only SBLF participants are required to submit these data. We excluded community development loan funds from the analysis as they are not regulated depository institutions, and the lack of supervisory information prevented us from describing comparable financial characteristics.

not assess banks' individual financial condition; rather, we looked at the medians of certain indicators to make comparisons between the four quartiles. We analyzed the financial condition of the SBLF banks in each of the four quartiles as of March 31, 2011, and June 30, 2013, to determine if any differences were associated with the initial financial condition of SBLF banks or changes in their financial condition that occurred during the program. To analyze the financial condition of the four quartiles, we accessed Call Report data using SNL Financial—a company that manages a financial database that contains publicly filed regulatory and financial reports.[3] To assess the factors associated with different lending levels, we used data from SNL Financial to analyze asset size, Texas Ratios, liquidity ratios, leverage ratios, wholesale funding, participation in Treasury's Capital Purchase Program (CPP), and geographic distribution for each of the four quartiles.[4] In addition, we calculated the net SBLF capital received using SNL Financial data and Treasury's Lending Growth Reports. We also obtained and analyzed CAMELS composite ratings from FDIC as of June 30, 2013, and March 31, 2011, to determine if there was variation across the quartiles.[5] Table 1 shows how the factor we analyzed varied by quartile as of June 30, 2013, and March 31, 2011.

---

[3]A Call Report is the common reference name for the quarterly reports of condition and income filed with regulators by every national bank, state-chartered Federal Reserve member bank, and insured state nonmember bank.

[4]As the largest capital infusion program under the Troubled Asset Relief Program, CPP was designed to provide capital investments to financially viable financial institutions. Treasury received preferred shares and subordinated debentures, along with warrants.

[5]The CAMELS rating system is a U.S. supervisory tool that describes a bank's overall condition and that is used to classify the nation's banks. The composite rating is based on financial statements and regulators' on-site examinations and has six components—capital adequacy, asset quality, management, earnings, liquidity, and sensitivity to market risk—that make up the acronym. It rates banks on a scale of 1 to 5, with 1 being the strongest.

Table 1: Aggregate Financial Health Information on SBLF Banks by Quartiles, as of March 31, 2011, and June 30, 2013

For the quarter ending June 30, 2013

	1st Quartile[a]	2nd Quartile	3rd Quartile	4th Quartile
Median asset size	$300,022	$390,442	$399,978	$602,114
Median Texas ratio[b]	7.23	9.85	14.72	19.17
Median liquidity ratio[c]	16.57	18.22	14.48	22.89
Median leverage ratio[d]	10.95	10.10	10.51	10.28
Median wholesale funding[e]	6.63	6.82	6.84	6.08
Median CAMELS score[f]	2	2	2	2

For the Quarter Ending March 31, 2011

	1st Quartile	2nd Quartile	3rd Quartile	4th Quartile
Median asset size	$217,767	$281,417	$361,676	$535,294
Median Texas ratio[b]	8.53	13.74	15.90	23.02
Median liquidity ratio[c]	17.96	20.03	16.67	21.28
Median leverage ratio[d]	10.04	9.12	8.97	9.42
Median wholesale funding[e]	6.58	7.38	7.13	6.57
Median CAMELS score[f]	2	2	2	2

Source: GAO analysis of Treasury, FDIC, and SNL Financial data.

[a]The figures in the table represent the median values for all banks in the particular quartile. SBLF banks in the first quartile had the highest level of qualified small business lending and growth in qualified small business lending compared to SBLF banks in the other three quartiles.

[b]The Texas ratio is defined as nonperforming assets ("troubled loans") plus loans 90 or more days past due divided by tangible equity and reserves.

[c]The liquidity ratio is defined as liquid assets divided by total liabilities.

[d]The leverage ratio is tier 1 capital divided by adjusted average assets.

[e]Reliance on wholesale funding depicts the portion of a bank's total funds that are from wholesale sources. Banks use wholesale funding sources to make up for the absence of local deposit funding, to provide greater flexibility in managing their asset/liability position, and to avoid the expenses associated with extensive branch networks.

[f]The CAMELS rating system is a U.S. supervisory tool that describes a bank's overall condition and that is used to classify the nation's banks. The composite rating is based on financial statements and regulators' on-site examinations and has six components—capital adequacy, asset quality, management, earnings, liquidity, and sensitivity to market risk—that make up the acronym. It rates banks on a scale of 1 to 5, with 1 being the strongest.

We assessed the reliability of the data used for our analyses by, for example, inspecting data for missing observations and outliers and reviewing prior GAO work and updating information as appropriate. We determined that the data collected by Treasury, FDIC, and SNL Financial we reviewed were sufficiently reliable for our purposes of providing a high-level overview of variations of changes in SBLF banks' qualified small business lending.

We also performed a regression analysis to assess the relationship
between variation in qualified small business lending levels and indicators
of banks' financial condition. Specifically, we analyzed the relationship
between qualified small business lending levels and the Texas Ratio,
reliance on wholesale funding, liquidity ratios, leverage ratios, net SBLF
capital received, state Gross Domestic Product (GDP), and participant-
reported demand for small business loans. We used financial measures
for SBLF banks that we have identified in prior reports to demonstrate an
institution's financial health as it relates to asset quality and capital
adequacy. We relied on SNL Financial for the Texas Ratio, reliance on
wholesale funding, liquidity ratios, leverage ratios, and net SBLF capital
received. We measured GDP in a state using data from the U.S.
Department of Commerce's Bureau of Economic Analysis. Finally, we
measured participant-reported demand for small business loans by using
responses from SBLF respondents to two questions in Treasury's first
annual SBLF survey and incorporated these responses through program
identifiers into our analysis.[6] We assessed the reliability of data from each
of these sources by, for example, inspecting data for missing
observations and outliers, reviewing prior GAO work, reviewing any
changes in survey methodologies, and updating information as
appropriate, and found the data to be sufficiently reliable for our
purposes. See appendix II for additional information on the regression
model.

To describe the reasons why some SBLF banks were more or less
successful in increasing lending to small businesses, we selected and
attempted to contact a nonprobability, judgmental sample of 12 banks
based on geographic distribution and participation in CPP. Specifically,
using the quartile breakdown we selected four banks from the first and
fourth quartiles (banks with the highest and lowest levels of qualified
small business lending) and two banks each from the second and third
quartiles. We first selected banks from each of six U.S. regions (Midwest,

---

[6]U.S. Department of the Treasury, *Results of the First Annual SBLF Lending Survey*, June
2013. The SBLF lending survey is an annual survey required by Treasury for all SBLF
participants as part of the agreement between Treasury and SBLF participants. The first
annual survey covered from July 1, 2011, to June 30, 2012. The questions to which we
obtained responses from banks on the demand for small business loans included, "How
has demand for overall small business lending changed over the past year?" and "At your
institution, how has the number of inquiries for new small business lending commitments
or increases in outstanding small business lending commitments changed over the past
year?"

West, Southeast, Southwest, Mid-Atlantic, and Northeast) and then
narrowed the selection to obtain a mix of prior CPP participants.[7] We
obtained responses from 10 of them. The results of these interviews
cannot be generalized to all SBLF banks but provide insights to reasons
for variation in lending.

To describe trends in small business credit markets and how these trends
may have affected a bank's ability to lend, we used a number of survey
indicators to describe market conditions as of June 2013 and before the
implementation of SBLF. These indicators included data from a survey
conducted by the National Federation of Independent Business on
whether members' borrowing needs are being satisfied; a survey by Wells
Fargo addressing banks' ease or difficulty in obtaining credit; and data
from the Federal Reserve Senior Loan Officer Opinion Survey on the
demand for credit across small firms and whether lending standards have
tightened or eased. We also relied on the results report of Treasury's first
SBLF annual survey. We also interviewed Treasury officials responsible
for the program and contacted representatives of the National Federation
of Independent Business, who regularly survey small businesses, and the
American Bankers Association and Independent Community Bankers
Association, who represent the interests of community banks. To
determine the reliability of these data sources, we interviewed company
representatives as appropriate to learn about their data collection
methods and any changes to their controls. We also reviewed previous
GAO work and survey methodologies to determine if there were any
changes made that would affect the data's reliability. Based on our
analysis we determined that, while the survey indicators were not
independently critical to our findings, they were sufficiently reliable
together to document patterns in the small business credit markets and
how these may affect a bank's ability to lend. To determine the reliability
of the Treasury survey data we used, we interviewed Treasury officials on

---

[7]The Midwest region includes Illinois, Indiana, Iowa, Kansas, Michigan, Minnesota,
Missouri, Nebraska, North Dakota, Ohio, South Dakota, and Wisconsin. The Northeast
region includes Connecticut, Maine, Massachusetts, and New Hampshire. The South
region includes Alabama, Arkansas, Delaware, District of Columbia, Florida, Georgia,
Kentucky, Louisiana, Maryland, Mississippi, North Carolina, Oklahoma, South Carolina,
Tennessee, Texas, Virginia, and West Virginia. The Southwest region includes parts of
Texas and Oklahoma, along with Arizona and New Mexico. The West region includes
Arizona, California, Colorado, Idaho, Montana, Nevada, Utah, Oregon, Washington, and
Wyoming. The Mid-Atlantic region includes Delaware, Maryland, New Jersey, New York,
Pennsylvania, and Washington, D.C.

their procedures for reviewing the survey responses, reviewed the nonresponse rate (none), and checked for consistency. Based on these steps, we determined that the data collected by Treasury were sufficiently reliable for the purpose of reporting on credit standards to SBLF banks.

Treasury's Evaluation of SBLF Lending

To determine actions Treasury has taken to evaluate SBLF participant lending patterns, we reviewed multiple Treasury documents, including the SBLF Lending Growth Reports issued in October 2012, and January, April, July, and October 2013, the first SBLF annual lending survey instrument, and the June 2013 results report for the first annual lending survey, as well as relevant supporting documentation of these reports. We also interviewed Treasury officials to understand the agency's efforts to assess program performance of SBLF. We also reviewed our 2011 and 2012 reports on SBLF to document Treasury's past efforts in assessing SBLF performance.[8] In addition, we reviewed GAO guidance on program evaluation and past GAO work on federal government performance management and compared Treasury's actions to this guidance and work.[9] Further, we reviewed impact evaluations conducted by other federal agencies and GAO to enhance our understanding and provide examples of impact analysis and statistical techniques.[10]

---

[8]GAO, *Small Business Lending Fund: Additional Actions Needed to Improve Transparency and Accountability*, GAO-12-183 (Washington, D.C.: Dec. 14, 2011) and *Small Business Lending: Opportunities Exist to Improve Performance Reporting of Treasury's Programs*, GAO-13-76 (Washington, D.C.: Dec. 5, 2012).

[9]See GAO, *Program Evaluation: A Variety of Rigorous Methods Can Help Identify Effective Interventions*, GAO-10-30 (Washington, D.C.: Nov. 23, 2009); *Performance Measurement and Evaluation: Definitions and Relationships*, GAO-11-646SP (Washington, D.C.: May 2011); *Designing Evaluations: 2012 Revision*, GAO-12-208G (Washington, D.C.: Jan. 2012); and *Program Evaluation: Strategies to Facilitate Agencies' Use of Evaluation in Program Management and Policy Making*, GAO-13-570 (Washington, D.C.: June 26, 2013).

[10]See GAO, *Tax Policy: New Markets Tax Credit Appears to Increase Investment by Investors in Low-Income Communities, but Opportunities Exist to Better Monitor Compliance*, GAO-07-296 (Washington, D.C.: Jan. 31, 2007); Social Policy Research Associates and Mathematica Policy Research, Inc., *Estimated Impacts for Participants in the Trade Adjustment Assistance (TAA) Program Under the 2002 Amendments* (August 2012); Urban Institute Justice Policy Center, *The Multi-Site Adult Drug Court Evaluation: The Impact of Drug Courts* (November 2011); and Institute of Education Sciences and Mathematical Policy Research, *Impacts of Title I Supplemental Educational Services on Student Achievement* (May 2012).

We conducted this performance audit from March 2013 to December 2013 in accordance with generally accepted government auditing standards. Those standards require that we plan and perform the audit to obtain sufficient, appropriate evidence to provide a reasonable basis for our findings and conclusions based on our audit objectives. We believe that the evidence obtained provides a reasonable basis for our findings and conclusions based on our audit objectives.

Appendix II: Econometric Model of Qualified Small Business Lending Growth at SBLF Banks

To help determine factors that may have influenced Small Business Lending Fund (SBLF) banks' ability to successfully translate SBLF equity into new lending we estimated a number of econometric models. We utilized information on SBLF banks' initial financial condition, Capital Purchase Program (CPP) conversion status, net capital received (netting out any equity used to repay Treasury CPP capital), state-level economic growth, and participant-reported small business loan demand.[1]

We first estimated a model based solely on the initial financial conditions as of March 31, 2011, of SBLF banks, using measures of equity, asset liquidity, reliance on wholesale funding, profitability, and troubled loans. All models were estimated via linear least squares with White heteroskedasticity-consistent standard errors.[2] We used two alternative measures of initial equity: the leverage ratio and the tier 1 risk-based capital ratio. We found that the leverage ratio was a somewhat stronger predictor (p-value =0.0009 vs. p-value = 0.0498) of growth in qualified small business lending, so we used that measure of equity in subsequent models. All other measures of financial conditions were statistically significant predictors of qualified small business lending growth with the exception of return on assets (a measure of profitability), which we excluded from subsequent models.

Next we added CPP conversion status to our model with financial conditions. CPP conversion status was a statistically significant predictor of qualified small business lending growth; however, once we add net capital to the model, CPP status was no longer statistically significant, while net capital was statistically significant (p-value =0.02). Because CPP conversion status and net capital are strongly negatively correlated, we excluded CPP status from subsequent models to avoid multicollinearity and associated variance inflation. After excluding CPP status from the model, the statistical significance of the net capital coefficient increased dramatically (p-value < 0.0001). These results suggest that net capital is driving differences between SBLF banks that

---

[1]As the largest capital investment program under the Troubled Asset Relief Program, CPP was designed to provide capital investments to financially viable financial institutions. Treasury received preferred shares and subordinated debentures, along with warrants. The initial capital that banks received from CPP was also intended to support lending.

[2]In all models we excluded a single outlier with extremely high qualified small business lending growth (19,471 percent over baseline). Several observations with missing data were also excluded.

paid off CPP capital with SBLF capital and other SBLF banks that did not, rather than an unobserved factor associated with CPP status.

To attempt to capture local economic conditions, we added state Gross Domestic Product (GDP) growth to the model with financial conditions and net capital. State GDP growth was not a statistically significant (p-value > 0.23) predictor of qualified small business lending growth. However, when we added a self-reported measure of demand for small business loans from Treasury's survey of SBLF participants to the model as an alternative, we found that this measure was a statistically significant predictor. These results suggest that state-level economic growth is not a precise measure of demand for loans at SBLF banks. We present the regression results of this final model in table 2 below. Because demand was self-reported, this variable could not be independently corroborated.[3] Participants with low growth in qualified small business lending may have had an incentive to report low demand to avoid the perception that they had underperformed. This tendency would cause our model to overstate the impact of local demand.

Table 2: Regression Model of Qualified Small Business Lending Growth, Baseline to First Quarter 2013

Variable	Coefficient	p-value
Leverage ratio[a]	0.06287	0.0023
Texas ratio[b]	-0.00961	< 0.0001
Liquidity ratio[c]	0.00905	0.0201
Wholesale funding[d]	0.03377	0.2141
Net capital[e]	9.1929	< 0.0001
Loan demand "same"[f]	0.20706	0.0082
Loan demand "stronger"[f]	0.23599	0.0004
R-squared	0.2759	NA

Source: GAO analysis of Treasury and SNL Financial data.

[a]The leverage ratio is tier 1 capital divided by adjusted average assets.

[b]The Texas ratio is defined as nonperforming assets ("troubled loans") plus loans 90 or more days past due divided by tangible equity and reserves.

[c]The liquidity ratio is defined as liquid assets divided by total liabilities.

---

[3]However, we did assess this variable for item nonresponse (none) and compared it to another measure of demand from the survey based on credit line inquiries, and found that it was strongly associated with this measure.

[d]Reliance on wholesale funding depicts the portion of a bank's total funds that are from wholesale sources. Banks use wholesale funding sources to make up for the absence of local deposit funding, to provide greater flexibility in managing their asset/liability position, and to avoid the expenses associated with extensive branch networks.

[e]Net capital received is the amount of capital received under SBLF netting out any equity used to repay Treasury Capital Purchase Program (CPP) capital.

[f]Responses based on U.S. Department of the Treasury, Results of the First Annual SBLF Lending Survey, June 2013, "How has demand for overall small business lending changed over the past year?"

The economic significance (magnitude) of some of these factors is summarized below:

- For every 14 percentage point increase in troubled loans (roughly one standard deviation) relative to capital and reserves, qualified small business lending growth decreased by 13 percentage points.

- For every 2 percentage points (roughly one standard deviation) more capital relative to assets (less leverage) prior to receiving SBLF capital, participants increased qualified small business lending by an additional 13 percentage points.

- A participant that received net SBLF capital of 1.9 percent (the mean) of assets relative to a participant that received no net capital (a potential outcome for participants that converted through CPP) increased qualified small business lending by an additional 18 percentage points.

- Participants that reported stronger demand for small business loans relative to those that reported weaker demand for small business loans increased qualified small business lending by an additional 24 percentage points.

Appendix III: Comments from the Department of the Treasury

DEPARTMENT OF THE TREASURY
WASHINGTON, D.C. 20220

December 5, 2013

Daniel Garcia-Diaz
Director
Financial Markets and Community Investment
U.S. Government Accountability Office
441 G Street, NW
Washington, DC 20548

Dear Mr. Garcia-Diaz:

Thank you for the opportunity to review the draft report entitled *Small Business Lending: Treasury Should Ensure Evaluation Includes Methods to Isolate Program Impact* (the Report). This letter provides the official response of the Department of the Treasury (Treasury).

The Report examines the Small Business Lend Fund (SBLF), a Treasury program established by the Small Business Jobs Act of 2010. Treasury is committed to informing the public and Congress about the outcomes of the SBLF program. We welcome GAO's conclusion that "Treasury has continued to develop and refine its approach to assessing the performance of SBLF and measuring the extent to which SBLF participants have increased small business lending."

As the Report notes, Treasury has employed multiple methods to evaluate the performance of SBLF including incorporating a peer analysis in the program's quarterly reports and conducting a lending survey of program participants. The results of these analyses suggest that SBLF banks have outperformed their peers and other community banks in increasing small business lending.

Treasury agrees that an impact evaluation may provide additional information with which to assess program performance and accepts GAO's recommendation to follow through in conducting this analysis. Treasury will complete this analysis using data from the conclusion of the program's two year incentive period – which concluded on September 30, 2013 – and anticipates publishing these results in FY 2014. Treasury will endeavor to develop analytical approaches to isolate further the program's role from other factors that could affect small business lending. Treasury notes that because the statistical technique of random assignment cannot be used in an impact evaluation to assess SBLF program impact, unmeasured factors may account for differences in lending growth between participants and comparison groups.

1

Thank you once again for the opportunity to review the Report. Treasury values GAO's review
of its programs and looks forward to continuing to work with your team.

Sincerely,

Don Graves
Deputy Assistant Secretary
Small Business, Community Development, and
Affordable Housing Policy

2

Appendix IV: GAO Contact and Staff Acknowledgments

GAO Contact	Daniel Garcia-Diaz, (202)-512-8678, garciadiazd@gao.gov.
Staff Acknowledgments	In addition to the individual named above, Kay Kuhlman (Assistant Director), Bethany Benitez, Anna Chung, Pamela Davidson, Patrick Dynes, Michael Hoffman, Lauren Nunnally, Jennifer Schwartz, and Jena Sinkfield made key contributions to this report.

GAO's Mission	The Government Accountability Office, the audit, evaluation, and investigative arm of Congress, exists to support Congress in meeting its constitutional responsibilities and to help improve the performance and accountability of the federal government for the American people. GAO examines the use of public funds; evaluates federal programs and policies; and provides analyses, recommendations, and other assistance to help Congress make informed oversight, policy, and funding decisions. GAO's commitment to good government is reflected in its core values of accountability, integrity, and reliability.
Obtaining Copies of GAO Reports and Testimony	The fastest and easiest way to obtain copies of GAO documents at no cost is through GAO's website (http://www.gao.gov). Each weekday afternoon, GAO posts on its website newly released reports, testimony, and correspondence. To have GAO e-mail you a list of newly posted products, go to http://www.gao.gov and select "E-mail Updates."
Order by Phone	The price of each GAO publication reflects GAO's actual cost of production and distribution and depends on the number of pages in the publication and whether the publication is printed in color or black and white. Pricing and ordering information is posted on GAO's website, http://www.gao.gov/ordering.htm. Place orders by calling (202) 512-6000, toll free (866) 801-7077, or TDD (202) 512-2537. Orders may be paid for using American Express, Discover Card, MasterCard, Visa, check, or money order. Call for additional information.
Connect with GAO	Connect with GAO on Facebook, Flickr, Twitter, and YouTube. Subscribe to our RSS Feeds or E-mail Updates. Listen to our Podcasts. Visit GAO on the web at www.gao.gov.
To Report Fraud, Waste, and Abuse in Federal Programs	Contact: Website: http://www.gao.gov/fraudnet/fraudnet.htm E-mail: fraudnet@gao.gov Automated answering system: (800) 424-5454 or (202) 512-7470
Congressional Relations	Katherine Siggerud, Managing Director, siggerudk@gao.gov, (202) 512-4400, U.S. Government Accountability Office, 441 G Street NW, Room 7125, Washington, DC 20548
Public Affairs	Chuck Young, Managing Director, youngc1@gao.gov, (202) 512-4800 U.S. Government Accountability Office, 441 G Street NW, Room 7149 Washington, DC 20548

Please Print on Recycled Paper.